Say It with a Haiku

俳句で伝える

Janice Whyne
ジャニス•ワイン

Say It with a Haiku

Cover design by WishartWorks
Cover art by WishartWorks © 2024 Rhoda Fisher

Publisher: Ashley Lawrence Ltd
ISBN: 978-0-9569235-7-8

Preface

In July 2021, I came across a YouTube clip of an interview with Lemn Sissay entitled, 'The importance of everyday acts of creativity.'[1] In it, Lemn mentioned creating short poems born out of whatever motivated or inspired him that morning.

The idea struck a chord, and I began writing a short poem every morning and posting it on Instagram. My first one, prompted by a pre-breakfast conversation with cousins, was called 'Eggs'.

I kept this up for a while and even set up a separate Instagram account, Daily_Poetics, to be a home for them.

[1] See Optional Extras for a QR code.

However, the usual suspects of a lack of discipline and life be lifing meant this daily act of creativity fizzled to a stop.

Fast forward to May 2023:
During a morning walk, some reeds on Covert Lane, Leicester, captured my attention.

Something about them made me reach out and touch them. I revelled in this touch of nature and envisioned a visual poem; I pressed record and enjoyed the moment again. Later that evening, a haiku emerged as the natural choice.

Then, in September 2023, a full-circle moment occurred. I attended Lemn Sissay's book launch of *Let the Light Pour In* at Foyles Charing Cross. Housed in this book are what he feels are the best of his morning poems.

The following morning, I wrote a short poem and (with a few exceptions) have written one every day since.

The morning after the night before.
no 24 robbers knocking at my door.
Rather, the rhythmic reflections of a
light-filled evening. Poured from
the soul of Sissay.

~ 20 Sept. 2023 | J M Whyne ~

It was the beginning of a commitment to write a haiku a day—desire to ensure that each day included an act of creativity.

After two weeks, I made an additional commitment; if this continued for 30 days, I would put out a book of Haiku.

I hope you enjoy this taste of my haiku journey thus far and that it might even encourage you to ***say it with a haiku.***

Janice
ジャニス•ワイン

An Invitation

Afforded by the morning

At your fingertips

~ 29 May 2023 | J M Whyne ~

A Touch of Nature

Why Haiku?

I chose to use Haiku because I had been exploring this form earlier in the year. I also felt the intrinsic brevity of a haiku naturally lent itself to the premise of the daily poem.

Writing a daily haiku enhances my creative practice.
I'm enjoying the freedom and challenge of packaging what I want to express in 17 syllables or less.

- It requires clarity and zeroing in on the main thing you want to say.
- It requires innovation, as you need to use fewer words and to find words that express more.
- It requires wordplay to hint at the deeper nuances within the brief lines.

Even when you can use more than 17 syllables, these apply.

This is probably a good place to say that **I am not a haiku expert** and would never purport to be.

I am an appreciator of the form who is learning as I go and whose appreciation has grown since attempting to write a haiku a day.

In general, I've used the 5-7-5 syllable rule and endeavoured to incorporate nature/seasonal references. I have, however, played with the format, where I felt this complemented the poem. For aesthetics, I've kept words whole that should technically (due to the syllable count) be hyphenated.

The haiku in this book are responses to everyday sights, sounds or occurrences. It can be amazing what we see if—in the words of Father James Martin SJ—we '**keep noticing**'.

They were also, at times, a reflection on what was happening in the world, such as in Gaza (2023). Linton Kwesi Johnson said ***writing was a political act and poetry was a cultural weapon.*** I have found poetry to be a means of protest.

Additional notes:

- I've shared 40 of what I consider to be some of my best (to date) haiku offerings, plus two Haibun offerings. As such, they appear in chronological, not consecutive, order.
- On some pages you will see QR codes, these will take you to visual versions of the corresponding haiku.
- While putting this book together, I realised that some of the poems are more akin to a senryu.[2]
- The Japanese calligraphy (book cover and title page) is courtesy of my friend and sis, Manami T. Uechi.
- All photographs, unless credited to others, were taken by me.

As I said in the preface, I hope you enjoy this taste of my haiku journey thus far and that it might encourage you to **begin your Haiku journey.**

---

[2] In short, the subject of the haiku is nature; the senryu, human nature." **Senryū: The Haiku's Comic Cousin***", Kimiko Hahn, poetrysociety.org***

Table of Contents

What is a Haiku?

A Japanese verse form most often composed, in English versions, of three unrhymed lines of five, seven, and five syllables. A haiku often features an image, or a pair of images, meant to depict the essence of a specific moment in time

Haiku (or hokku) | Poetry Foundation[1]

Book Title: Japanese Translation

俳句で伝える（Haiku de Tsutaeru)

Since Haiku is a poetic form which originated in Japan, it felt right to reflect/pay homage to this in the title. I am blessed to have been able to ask my friend Manami (aka lil sis) to help me with this. She shared the following:

> "Japanese translation is a bit tricky because we have to translate it creatively instead of literally. I'd suggest we use 俳句で伝える, which sounds a bit more formal, succinct, and professional.
>
> The Google translate, 俳句で伝えよう, on the other hand, sounds more friendly and it's more conversational, meaning you are talking to/suggesting to someone that you **"deliver your message through haiku together"** (informal colloquial Japanese use)

It sounds almost like...

"Let's express in haiku together."

No. 1

Seeds of connection
Sown—watered—blossoming blooms
Ripe for harvest now

21 September 2023

No. 4

Fallow unbroken
ground, just beneath the surface,
newness awaiting.

24 September 2023

No. 6

Summer's silhouette

still dances between the looming

Autumn shadows

26 September 2023

No. 8

Like a gust of air
meaningful moments pass swiftly
lasting lifetimes

28 September 2023

No. 13

Like the low rumble
of distant thunder, so it
is with transition.

3 October 2023

No. 16

Day and night. What lies
between them can't be contained
in a conjunction.

6 October 2023

No. 17

To be present—the

priceless gift all can afford

to give and receive

7 October 2023

No. 19

Transported back in

time, its green leaves revealed

untold stories from home.

9 October 2023[3]

The Power of
the Banana Tree

[3] This haiku was inspired by a moment shared with my Mum during a visit to the Royal Botanic Gardens, Kew. A day out for her birthday. Scan the QR to read the journal post which it also inspired.

No. 23

Strewn like leaves on the

ground, but not as nature

intended it to be.

12 October 2023

Fallen Leaves

(Haibun[4] – an extension of No. 23)

The rust vision of them began in thought before deed. Walking at speed to make that connection. Drawn to a halt by the call of the leafy kaleidoscope. Silently adorning the grey-red brick road.

With hints of green and branches laid bare, it was hard not to stare and keep looking ahead. As late as it would make me, the sight of them compelled me.

This was their last act. The curtain had fallen, no longer attached to their life-giving source. They had come to their natural conclusion.

---

[4] Japanese poet **Matsuo Basho** created this poetic form in which a poet combines prose and haiku to create a prose poem. The prose poem typically describes a setting, scene, or moment in an objective manner and follows the standard formal considerations of **haiku.- poetryfoundation.org/learn/glossary-terms/haibun**

Falling like leaves, strewn
on the ground, but this was not
an act of nature.

13 October 2023

Fallen Leaves

No. 24

Saturday's sun shooed
rain away. Don't worry said
Rain, I'll come again.

14 October 2023

No. 26

Light beckons from behind

the curtains, inviting

you to open up.

16 October 2023

No. 27

A world possessed with

more arms than sense,

humanity feels on the brink.

17 October 2023

No. 27a

Saluting Our Sisters[5]

5 "We are here!" Voices

calling from the footnotes. Look

closely and you'll see.

17 October 2023

No. 36

A touch of beauty

amidst the monstrous landscape;

momentary peace.

26 October 2023

No. 37

Precious baubles
adorning green leaves;
soon, this gift will drop to the ground.

27 October 2023

No. 40

First ting in da

morning ting, do my prayers

centre my mind and ting.

30 October 2023

No. 41

Present and Past shadow boxing:

jab

cross

left hook

uppercut

impact.

31 October 2023

No. 43

Caught in a contact-

less world. How high the price

of innovation.

2 November 2023

No. 45

How is it for you?

Every shiver amplified,

calls me to prayer.

4 November 2023

No. 46

Slow tears run today

laden by gravity

fallen humanity

5 November 2023

"Not all tears are alike. The human body produces three kinds: basal, which form an oily layer over the eyeball to keep it from drying out; ...and psychogenic, which are shed for emotional reasons. Notably, emotional tears have a higher protein level than basal and reflex tears, which makes them thicker and causes them to fall more slowly."[6]

- Heather Christle

Why Do We Cry?

[6] Why do we cry and what can we learn from our tears? *Heather Christle,* ***Guardian.com****, 8 February 2020*

No. 48

Encased in a tear
Grief wider than oceans
A silent tsunami

5 November 2023

No. 49

Will they fly kites again?
Now breaking world records
of a different kind.[7]

6 November 2023

[7] On July 29 2011, during an event by **UNRWA**, children of the Gaza strip broke the **Guinness world record** for most kites flown simultaneously.

No. 50

Eyes cannot un-see

Ears cannot un-hear

Unfinished Haiku | 8 November 2023[8]

---

[8] After wrestling to find an ending which fit the traditional syllable count, I posted it with this caption, ***An unfinished #haiku or maybe it already says what it needs to.***

No. 51

(the continuation)[9]

Eyes cannot un-see

Ears cannot un-hear

...Our hearts cannot turn away.

...We can't choose to turn away.

...They can't choose to turn away.

...Out of our hearts the mouth speaks.

...We are called to bear witness.

Eyes cannot un-see.

Ears cannot un-hear.

The un-heard of is happening there.

8 November 2023

[9] The unfinished haiku eventually had a few endings. They were responses to news from Gaza.

No. 54

Remnants of joy dusting
our days and soothing
salt-stained cheeks

10 November 2023

No. 55

Chasing truth like the
sunflower chasing the sun
Drawn into its rays

11 November 2023

No. 56

Misunderstandings
like fault lines - deepening the
divide between us

11 November 2023

No. 61

I like the blue roses.

I do, too. How vibrant

the colours of grief.

16 November 2023

No. 68

From today's ashes,

thankfulness. A daily act

of resistance.

23 November 2023

No. 72

A wor ÷ ld humanity subtracted = current times

27 November 2023

Haiku No. 72

No. 81

Shades of grey above

Inclement times are coming

Yet light still endures

5 December 2023

No. 85

They walk amoung us

Those erased from history.

show us our future

9 December 2023

No. 94

Rising with the sun
is a gift. What will you give
in return?

19 December 2023

Photo courtesy of **Morlene Fisher**

No. 100

'Mixed Feelings': Christmas Day 2023

(Haibun offering no.2)

Tis the time of year for mixing:
seasonings, company, feelings.

Prepping in my onesie, but not alone.
Thinking of those whose only companion is loneliness.

Living between homes, yet thinking of those who have no place to lay their head.

In need of solace, seeking shelter, "no room at the inn" a familiar story.

Grateful for family, near and far. Aware of those who are absent and those who will never be forgotten.

Thinking of those who do not know the love of family or those separated by

distance
displacement
and a divided world

Dressed in red, fitting for the occasion. Thinking of those robed in the red of martyred loved ones.

Taken from this world,
by those whose blood must run cold

Listening to the songs about the Saviour, the reason for the season, the refugee Saviour.

Wondering what songs are being sung in occupied lands? Lands which house the choirs of Ancestors.

Holding the tension between the now and not yet—the what is and what it should be.

Tis the season of
mixed feelings, our joy and our
need of redemption.

No. 107

You and the New Year

Yet to be acquainted

Give it some time

1 January 2023

No. 113

That which can be known,

let it be known. Life with one

less mystery.

7 January 2024

No. 118

Temperatures rising

lava erupting - Lovers

to your corners.

16 January 2024

No. 119

Home sweet home, soured

by the suspects in blue.

There's no place like home.

17 January 2024

No. 120

Wait your turn / All in
good time / Sometimes we need
to step out of line

18 January 2024

No. 130

Long-distance decisions

dividing the world, degrees

of separation.[10]

29 January 2023

[10] I broke the usual haiku convention of 17 syllables, as I liked the alliteration of keeping the word 'decisions'

No. 132

Hope persists in the

broken-hearted, like the sun

breaking through the clouds.

1 February 2024

Photo courtesy of **James Beard** // Glimmer // Lyme Regis, Dorset, UK

No. 135

Barren limbs all a
quiver, they know their wait will
soon be over.

4 February 2024

About the Author

Since childhood, Janice Whyne has been a words person, writing prose-filled Christmas cards, songs and poetry. She sees poetry as a conduit for our individual and collective feelings and lived experiences.

She's a Londoner by birthplace, a Jamaican by birthright, and regards Indonesia—where she worked as a community development worker for ten years—as another homeland.

Say It with a Haiku is her 2nd poetry book. As well as the poetry book, there is a *Say It with a Haiku* journal – a place to house your poems and poetic musings.

Her debut poetry book, *In Conversation,*[77] was published in 2022 and was a personal milestone in Janice's journey of rediscovering her creative self. It's a collection of poems touching on themes of life, loss, love, protest and more.

As well as writing poetry, Janice is a spoken word artist. She was 1st runner-up at the Ubud Writers & Readers Festival Poetry Slam (2019 & 2022) and has

[77] Available from Amazon worldwide & partner retailers (paperback, eBook & audiobook - all major platforms). Scan the QR code to get yours.

performed at Flovortex, The Mother Wolf Club, Voices in Power - London, Poets Palace plus various other venues and functions.
You can view some of her poetry, spoken word performances and other content via her socials (see below for details).

Her poem 'Sitting with Amazing' is in The Poetry Archive Now Worldview 2021 Winners collection. Other poems appear in 'Coffee & Contemplation: a taste of empowerment' (2020), Coffee People Zine, Issue 10 (2020), All My Relations, Vol. 5, Talbot-Heindl (2023), 'Her locks unveiled: poems from the Black in White poetry competition' (2023) as well as in other online and printed mediums.

If you are interested in booking Janice for your event or to facilitate a poetry workshop for your group, team or organisation, contact her via her website: www.janicewhyne.com. You can also contact and follow her via social media or LinkedIn:

IG: @jjsmuse

FB: JJ s Muse

YT: @janichay

LI: Janice Whyne

In Conversation
Amazon

The Story Behind the Cover

A picture Janice sent me a while back, standing with her arms outstretched as her homestay family dresses her in a Yukata (浴衣)[12], was a powerful inspiration for a book cover.

In her Yukata, Janice fully embraces her host culture while peacefully engrossed in a book, a beautiful and evocative image that can be a powerful inspiration for a book cover.

The Yukata, a traditional Japanese garment, symbolises Janice's connection to her host culture, while her serene expression conveys a sense of contentment and belonging.

Where else would I place my cousin but reading a book amid blooming cherry blossoms in the land of the rising sun?

WishartWorks (Rhoda Fisher)

---

[12] Yukata 浴衣, Japan-Gudie.com

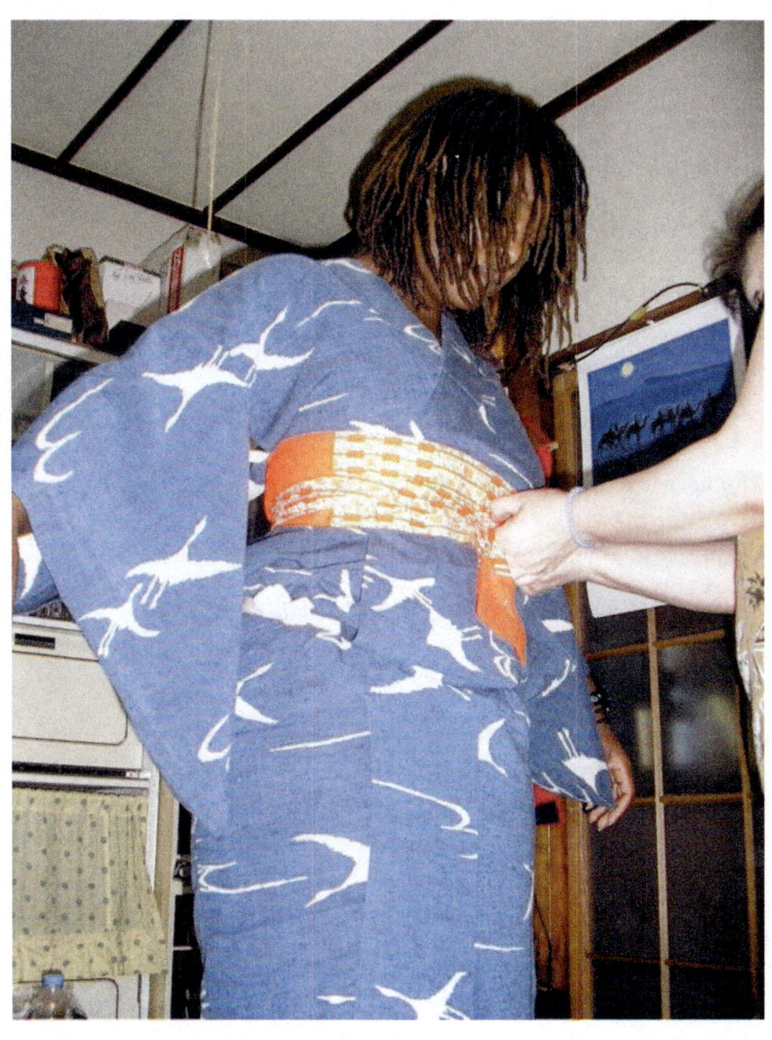

Acknowledgements

To the Creator and Author of my life, I am grateful for the words and opportunity You have gifted to me.

To Mum and Dad, thank you for your consistent, loving presence in my life. To G, love you, my brother. I couldn't ask for a better sibling. To Donovan and Gabrielle, you know how much your Aunty loves you, and I am proud of you.

To my extended family, thank you for the love, laughter (aka bare jokes!), and support you bring to my life. **Special thanks** to my Aunts, Uncles, and Grandparents (past & present). You paved the way for us, sometimes through great trials. *I (we) are the success of the seeds you have sown.*

To my god-children, you have made your mark in my life and are making your mark on the world. I am proud of you.

To my Tribe - my sisters - I love and appreciate you.

To James Beard and Morlene Fisher, thank you for letting me use your evocative photography. Additional thanks to Morlene, for making my photos pop!

To WishartWorks (aka cousin Rhoda), your cover art is breathtakingly gorgeous. **Thank you** for pouring so much into it.

To Manami T. Uechi (aka lil sis), thank you for the beautiful Japanese calligraphy. It was an extra special touch.

Finally, to you, dear readers. Firstly, to those who read my draft(s): Thank you for your time, feedback and for helping me with the challenging task of selecting the haiku housed in this book.

Secondly, to you reading this now and who have—or are about to—*Say It with a Haiku,* **thank you.**

Janice
ジャニス•ワイン

Optional Extras

- My JJ's Muse Linktree, where you can access links to my online content I.e. performances, books, merchandise (t-shirts, mugs), across different platforms.

- Lemn Sissay, "The importance of everyday acts of creativity." YouTube clip and corresponding article.

Sissay clip

- What is a Haiku?
    - Poets.org

What is a

- The Topography of Tears: Rose-Lynn Fisher

The Topography of Tears

- My Haiku video playlists
    - YouTube

Haiku Playlist - YT

- My Poetry & Spoken word playlist

Poetry & Spoken word

Printed in Great Britain
by Amazon